HANNAH G. SOLOMON

DARED TO MAKE A DIFFERENCE

To my writer-husband Martin, daughter-teacher Shamira, to
Antonia Lavine and Linda Kurtz, NCJW friends who supported
my dream of publishing this book, and to all readers who dare
to make a difference in our world. –B.L.

To Aleksandr Egorov, my first and only art teacher –S.M.

The author is indebted to the Jewish Women's Archive for access to Hannah G. Solomon's autobiography,
The Fabric of My Life: The Autobiography of Hannah G. Solomon, accessed August 27, 2020, and additional
archival material on Hannah Greenebaum Solomon, accessed August 26, 2020, https://jwa.org/
womenofvalor/solomon.

KAR-BEN PUBLISHING®
An imprint of Lerner Publishing Group, Inc.
241 First Avenue North
Minneapolis, MN 55401 USA
Website address: www.karben.com

Main body text set in Baskerville Com Regular.
Typeface provided by Linotype AG.

Library of Congress Cataloging-in-Publication Data

The Cataloging-in-Publication Data for *Hannah G. Solomon Dared to Make a Difference* is on file at the Library
of Congress.
ISBN 978-1-72841-573-4 (lib. bdg.)
ISBN 978-1-72841-574-1 (pbk.)
ISBN 978-1-72842-892-5 (eb pdf)

Manufactured in the United States of America
1-48687-49105-11/24/2020

HANNAH G. SOLOMON
DARED TO MAKE A DIFFERENCE

Bonnie Lindauer

Illustrated by Sofia Moore

KAR-BEN
PUBLISHING

HANNAH G. SOLOMON'S city was buzzing with activity. This year, 1893, the Columbian Exposition would be held in Chicago, Illinois. People would come from all over to attend this magnificent fair. It would transform Hannah's frontier town into a glamorous destination known around the world.

In 1893, the Columbian Exposition, later known as the Chicago World's Fair, attracted 27 million people from around the world. They visited impressive buildings and gardens created especially for the fair, and they saw art exhibitions and new inventions like the Ferris wheel.

The fair's planning committee invited Hannah to organize events for Jewish women during the fair. They knew Hannah was good at overseeing people and programs.

Hannah was nervous. She had never handled a project this big before. The job would be a challenge. But it was also an exciting opportunity. She wanted women from all over the country to attend the fair, meet one another, and join forces to do good in the world.

Hannah's interest in helping others began in her childhood. Her parents had come to the United States from Germany. Her father was a volunteer firefighter and a founder of the first Reform synagogue in Chicago. He also helped new immigrants find jobs. Hannah's mother started Chicago's first Jewish Ladies' Sewing Society, making clothes for the poor.

Hannah's parents taught her that everyone deserved freedom and respect.

Hannah's father, Michael Greenebaum, taught Hannah that American slavery—the practice of white people owning Black people as property—was wrong. Slavery was not legal in the state of Illinois, but according to the law, white people in every state were supposed to help capture any enslaved people who ran away from their owners. Hannah's father refused to follow this law.

When a man fleeing slavery was captured in Chicago, Hannah's father helped him to escape from jail. The Civil War ended legal slavery in the United States in 1865, when Hannah was five.

When Hannah was thirteen, an enormous fire swept through Chicago. "All through the night," she wrote later, "we stood at the windows and watched the flames and smoke—all of us fully dressed so that we might be ready to flee to the prairies if the fire came our way." Her family's home was spared from the fire, but many others were not so lucky.

"My parents opened our house to the homeless, filling it to capacity," Hannah remembered. The people of Chicago rebuilt their city, but Hannah never forgot the pain she'd seen among people who had lost everything.

The Great Chicago Fire of 1871 burned for two days, killed 300 people, destroyed more than 3 square miles of Chicago, and left more than 100,000 people homeless.

As Hannah grew up, she realized that many people in Chicago were suffering. Thousands of Jews from Russia and Poland lived in poor neighborhoods, struggling to survive. Often, several families had to cram into a tiny two-room apartment. In the winter, frigid air seeped in through the poorly constructed, badly heated buildings. This caused health problems.

Many immigrants didn't speak English and didn't have enough education to get good jobs. Instead, they worked in dangerous conditions for very low pay. Many families didn't have enough to eat.

Hannah wanted to help. She and her sister Henriette were the first Jewish women to be elected to the Chicago Women's Club, an important community service group. Her work with this group got her noticed by the World's Fair planners.

Now, Hannah was in charge of bringing Jewish women to the fair. "The task confronting me appeared colossal," Hannah remembered later. "Somehow, some way, I must gather together America's outstanding Jewish women. But how could I go about it . . . ?"

At first, Hannah tried to team up with the group planning Jewish men's activities. But these men didn't want women to play a major part in the fair. Many men thought women should focus only on being wives and mothers, instead of having big plans and ideas.

Hannah joked to her friends, "The only part of the program they wished us to fill was the chairs."

But Hannah didn't give up. "I must show them what a woman can do!" she thought.

She wrote letters to leading rabbis all over the country, asking them to send her names of outstanding women in their congregations. Then she wrote to each woman on the rabbis' lists, inviting them all to participate in a Jewish women's conference at the World's Fair.

The conference speakers would talk about important issues, like education and equality. Hannah believed women should care about these issues. She hoped the speakers could come up with ways to improve people's lives.

Hannah's family encouraged her. Her children even helped stuff the invitation letters into the envelopes.

On September 4, 1893, the conference began. Over four days, notable Jewish women gave speeches to an overflowing audience. The event was a huge success.

Near the end of the conference, Hannah spoke. She had an idea.

There should be a permanent Jewish women's group that worked to help people around the country.

The National Council of Jewish Women was born, and Hannah became its first president.

Hannah knew that not everyone would support the NCJW, as the organization became known. Many people believed that women were not cut out to be leaders, and might neglect their husbands and children. Hannah warned the other women to be prepared for criticism.

She insisted that women could make a difference in the world, if they dared to try.

The NCJW focused on Jewish education and on helping people in need, especially women and children. Members gathered clothing and supplies for Jewish immigrants who had almost nothing. They created workrooms to train poor women for jobs.

Under Hannah's leadership, the NCJW helped convince local leaders to pass new laws that would help the community. These laws gave people better housing, started the first free public nursery school, and created public playgrounds for children. Hannah also made sure that poor children could get meals at school. She wanted all children to have safe places to grow, play, and learn.

Hannah also wanted poor women to have chances to improve their lives. She volunteered at Hull House, a community center started by her friend, Jane Addams, where immigrant women could take classes, learn job skills, and socialize.

Hannah also helped start another community center, the Maxwell Street Settlement House, specifically for Jewish immigrants.

With Jane Addams, Susan B. Anthony, and others, Hannah spoke out in favor of women's rights. She believed women should be able to vote in elections, just as men did.

WE HAVE VOICE

Hannah's friend, Susan B. Anthony, had started
fighting for women's rights before Hannah was even born.

The 19th Amendment was passed by Congress in 1919 and ratified in 1920, granting many American women the right to vote. Hannah celebrated, knowing that voting would give women new ways to make a difference in their own lives and the lives of others.

But Hannah's work wasn't finished. There was still much to be done.

Hannah G. Solomon continued to make the world better, especially for women and children, throughout her life.

AUTHOR'S NOTES

ABOUT HANNAH G. SOLOMON

Hannah Greenebaum Solomon has been called Chicago's most important Jewish leader of her generation. She founded and led the first national association for Jewish women, whose actions redefined the roles of women in American society. Her legacy is celebrated by the organization she founded, the National Council of Jewish Women. The NCJW currently has 90,000 members in 62 sections around the country. The organization's goal is the same as Hannah's was: "Improve the quality of life for women, children and families and . . . ensure individual rights and freedoms for all."

The Hannah G. Solomon Elementary School in Chicago was named after Hannah, and she is also honored on New Jersey's Hannah G. Solomon Day every January 14.

ABOUT HULL HOUSE

Hannah's friend Jane Addams was born in 1860, two years after Hannah's birth. In 1889, Jane and Ellen Gates Starr started Hull House, a settlement house for poor immigrant women. Some women lived in the house, while thousands of others visited. The house had a school for adults, clubs for children, an art gallery, a library, and music and theater groups. Most poor people had never had access to these things before.

TIMELINE

1858: Hannah Greenebaum is born on January 14.

1861–1865: The Civil War splits the nation.

1871: The Great Chicago Fire devastates the city.

1876: Hannah and her sister Henriette become the first Jewish members of the Chicago Women's Club.

1879: Hannah marries Henry Solomon.

1893: Hannah organizes the first Jewish Women's Congress, which is held at the Chicago World's Fair, and founds the National Council of Jewish Women, becoming its first president.

1897: Hannah founds the Bureau of Personal Service to help Jewish immigrants.

1904: Hannah and her friend Susan B. Anthony travel to Berlin, Germany, to attend a meeting of the International Council of Women, a women's rights group.

1905: Hannah retires and is named honorary NCJW president for life.

1907: Hannah serves as president of the Illinois Industrial School for Girls, which provides job training for young women.

1910: Hannah chairs the Chicago Waste Agency, working to make the city cleaner and healthier.

1917–1918: During World War I, Hannah chairs a group of Chicago's neighborhood leaders, organizing community efforts to support American soldiers.

1920: The 19th Amendment to the Constitution is adopted. It gives women the right to vote, although many women of color were not able to vote until laws changed in later decades.

1942: Hannah dies on December 7 at the age of 84.

ABOUT THE AUTHOR

A former high school teacher and college librarian, Bonnie Lindauer loves reading children's books as much as she loves her favorite vanilla ice cream. She plays piano and cello, and loves to sing. She lives near San Francisco with her husband and senior rescue dog, Archie. This is her first children's book.

ABOUT THE ILLUSTRATOR

Sofia Moore is a Ukrainian American artist and illustrator based in Las Vegas. She grew up reading folktales in her grandmother's house and drawing princesses on the back of textbooks. She loves painting traditionally but also layers textures both on paper and digitally.

PHOTO ACKNOWLEDGMENTS

Photos on page 30 are courtesy of The Jacob Rader Marcus Center of the American Jewish Archives, Cincinnati, Ohio, at americanjewisharchives.org (portrait); Thomas Barrat/Shutterstock.com (Hull House).